in the Lord

"There are many lengthy and complex volumes written on St. Augustine. But this little book takes us right to the heart of Augustine's spirituality. Mattingly's invitation to pray with St. Augustine will help you to experience the warmth, ardent love for God, and zeal for the neighbor that are the hallmarks of Augustine's spiritual vision—and to discover in St. Augustine a new spiritual friend."

John Cavadini

Director of the McGrath Institute for Church Life
University of Notre Dame

"St. Augustine is easily one of the most influential writers and thinkers in the history of Christendom. For more than 1600 years, the saints and sinners who came after him have connected with his theological profundity, finding in his works a pathway to their own sanctity and spiritual growth. What a gift *Rejoice in the Lord* is to the modern Church, opening up a whole new generation of believers to the passion and zeal of this spiritual giant. This little book will bless countless souls in their pursuit of God."

Mark Hart

Executive vice president of Life Teen International

Rejoice in the Lord

Augustine of Hippo

Edited by Trenton W. Mattingly

Ave Maria Press · Ave · Notre Dame, Indiana

Series Editor: John Kirvan

For this work, early translations of various writings of Augustine of
Hippo, primarily *Confessions*, *Meditations*, as well as his *Expositions on
the Psalms* have been distilled, freely adapted into modern English,
combined, rearranged, and paraphrased into a meditational format.

© 2021 by Ave Maria Press, Inc.

Founded in 1865, Ave Maria Press is a ministry of the United States
Province of Holy Cross.

www.avemariapress.com

Paperback: ISBN-13 978-1-64680-043-8

E-book: ISBN-13 978-1-64680-044-5

Cover image © gettyimages.com.

Cover and text design by Katherine Robinson.

Printed and bound in the United States of America.

Library of Congress Cataloging-in-Publication Data is available.

CONTENTS

TIMELINE *vii*

WHO IS AUGUSTINE OF HIPPO? 1

HOW TO PRAY THIS BOOK 7

THIRTY DAYS WITH AUGUSTINE OF HIPPO 15

ONE FINAL WORD 95

TIMELINE

354   Augustine is born on November 13 in
           Thagaste in the province of Numidia in
           North Africa (modern-day Algeria). His
           father, Patricius, was a pagan, and his
           mother, Monica, was a Christian.

354–365   Patricius, recognizing his son's intellectual
           gifts, makes significant financial sacrifices
           to secure a classical Latin education for
           Augustine.

366–370   Augustine's education continues at
           Madaura.

371–373   Augustine's father dies, and Augustine
           moves to Carthage (which he would later
           describe as "a cauldron of illicit loves")
           to continue his education. It is here that
           Augustine begins a thirteen-year rela-
           tionship with a concubine, with whom he
           has a son named Adeodatus. Also during
           this time, Augustine begins to follow
           Manichaeism.

373   Upon reading Cicero's *Hortensius*, Augus-
           tine becomes awakened to a desire for true
           wisdom and devotes himself to philosophi-
           cal study.

374   Augustine begins his teaching career,
           returning to his hometown of Thagaste to
           teach grammar and rhetoric.

376	After the death of a close friend, Augustine returns to Carthage where he opens a school of rhetoric.
379	Theodosius I becomes emperor of the Roman Empire, ruling until 395. During this time, Orthodox Christianity is established as the official state religion of the Roman Empire.
381	The Council of Constantinople is convened.
383	With his concubine and son, Augustine sails to Rome.
384	Augustine moves to Milan, where he takes up an intense study of the Neoplatonists and becomes a professor of rhetoric. It is here that Augustine encounters the compelling teaching influence of Bishop Ambrose.
386	Following a period of intense conflict between his carnal appetites and his spiritual impulse toward truth, Augustine undergoes a powerful conversion experience.
387	Returning to Milan, Augustine and his son are baptized by Bishop Ambrose; shortly afterward, at Ostia, Augustine and his mother, Monica, have a shared "vision." Monica dies at Ostia.

388–390	Following further travels to Rome, Carthage, and Thagaste, Augustine's son dies.
391	Restless with grief and filled with a desire to serve, Augustine visits Hippo. Bishop Valerius, facing an urgent need for Catholic ministers, prevails upon Augustine to accept ordination as a priest. Augustine spends the rest of his life ministering and writing in Hippo.
392–395	Augustine publicly debates Fortunatus the Manichee and engages in deeper study of scripture, requesting that Jerome send Latin translations of Bible commentaries. Augustine also combats the Donatists, arguing against their elitist vision of Christianity.
396	Augustine becomes bishop of Hippo.
ca. 400	Augustine writes his *Confessions*; at about the same time (390–405), Jerome translates the Bible into the Latin Vulgate.
ca. 403–412	Augustine combats the Donatist heresy.
412–421	Augustine combats the Pelagian heresy.
413–427	In a period of astonishing literary output, Augustine writes *The City of God*, *On the Trinity*, *The Enchiridion*, and his *Retractions*.
430	On August 28, Augustine dies, at the age of seventy-five.

1298   Pope Boniface VIII elevates the feast of Augustine of Hippo as a Doctor of the Church.

WHO IS
AUGUSTINE OF HIPPO?

The titles that rightly belong to Augustine of Hippo are many: sinner, scholar, saint, convert, successor to the apostles, Church Father, and Doctor of the Church. As you might imagine, it would be difficult to overstate the extent of his influence—both within the Church as a masterful theologian and beyond the Church thanks to his work in philosophy and political theory. Those familiar with Augustine in his early years might not have guessed he was destined for sainthood. And yet, his winding spiritual journey was marked at every step by his heart's restless yearning for the divine—a quality that would eventually find vital expression in his vast literary output and continues to inspire Christian thought and devotion.

Augustine was born in AD 354 in Thagaste, a small Roman community located in modern-day Algeria. His parents were not particularly well-off, but they were free Roman citizens, a status that brought several societal advantages, including the opportunity to provide the young Augustine with an excellent education. Augustine's mother, Monica, was a devout Christian who sought to raise her children in the Catholic faith. But Augustine, despite being a pre-baptismal candidate as a young child, turned away from Christianity in his teenage years, embarking instead on a lengthy exploration of various religious and philosophical systems. Monica began to pray fervently that Augustine would one day return to the faith she had raised him in, but it would be many years before her prayers were answered.

Augustine, building on the foundation of his excellent early education, became devoted to academic pursuits in his young adult years, leading to a formative encounter with the work of a Roman statesman and academic named Cicero. Though Augustine ultimately found Cicero's ideas lacking, they awakened within him a passionate desire to search for truth and wisdom. Augustine briefly examined Christianity, the faith of his youth, but he was unimpressed. Rather, he found himself drawn into a decade-long involvement with Manichaeism, a dualistic religious system that professed to be deeply rooted in reason. During this period in Augustine's life, he continued a relationship with a concubine he had taken when he was seventeen years old, had a son with her, became deeply entrenched in his attachments to sexual sin, and aggressively pursued lofty secular and academic ambitions with much success.

Augustine quickly rose to prominence, gaining a reputation as a skilled rhetorician. In his early twenties, he already was serving as a professor of rhetoric in Carthage. Despite the prestigious nature of the position, Augustine found it unsatisfying and was disappointed with the quality of his students. Even so, while in this role—and despite living a rather hedonistic lifestyle—Augustine continued to study and search for truth. His search made him increasingly skeptical of Manichaeism. Despite its lofty claims of enlightenment, its prophet Mani's philosophical framework could not answer Augustine's deepest questions or stand up against key criticisms. After an incredibly disappointing meeting with a renowned and highly regarded Manichean bishop, Augustine entered a religious crisis and began to withdraw from many of his long-held assumptions and beliefs.

Shortly after a move to Milan to accept another prestigious teaching position, Augustine abandoned his belief in Manichaeism entirely. In this new season of searching, he started attending the sermons of Bishop Ambrose of Milan. At first, he was simply impressed by the bishop's prowess in rhetoric and oration. But gradually, Augustine found himself becoming interested in the actual content of the sermons. Ambrose's words re-introduced Christianity to Augustine's hungry soul, merging with Augustine's own search for truth, his mother Monica's persistent prayers, and even a divine intervention from God that encouraged Augustine to take and read sacred scripture. All these factors led Augustine, finally, to the Catholic Church. Although it was an enormous struggle to give up his past life of pleasure-seeking and worldly ambition, Augustine humbled himself and was baptized by Ambrose.

Augustine eventually returned to Africa and, much to his chagrin, continued to develop a following. But, this time, his reputation was based not only on his sharp intellect and skill as a rhetorician but also on his piety and radical devotion to his faith. In fact, Augustine's popularity was so great that a mob of admirers seized him, dragged him before a bishop, and demanded his immediate ordination to the priesthood. Augustine humbly relented and was ordained. He was consecrated as a bishop just a few years later.

During his episcopacy, Augustine was widely regarded as a great, confident leader. He fought passionately against heresy, was a devoted student of sacred scripture, and did his best to lovingly guide his flock to deep, authentic relationships with Christ. Augustine was also particularly invested in rebutting various pagan critiques of Christianity and the false claims made by Donatism and Pelagianism, two popular heresies of his time. During this period in his life, Augustine also produced writings that would have massive, lasting influence on the development of Christian doctrine, including *The City of God, On the Trinity,* and his spiritual autobiography, *Confessions.*

Each of these writings reveals in its own way that Augustine was not only a brilliant scholar, insightful thinker, and poetic writer—he was above all a passionate lover of God. Faith was not just an intellectual endeavor for Augustine; it was an authentic relationship with— and a deep, abiding love for—the God of the universe. This relationship was imprinted deeply on his heart and provided a lens for all of his thoughts and actions. Given this intimacy with God, perhaps it should come as no surprise that prayers and devotions are woven throughout even the most densely theological and philosophical of Augustine's writings. He wanted others to experience the love of God too. Possessed of a deep understanding of the human condition, the addictive and harmful nature of sin and temptation, and the struggles and anxieties of our existence, Augustine acknowledged that we cannot truly be whole until we learn to rest in God.

The purpose of this book, then, is to invite you into an authentic experience of St. Augustine's spirituality. It is our sincere hope and prayer that this thirty-day devotional will teach you to pray as St. Augustine of Hippo did, bringing you closer to God, and helping you along your Christian journey. Most of all, we hope you will rejoice in the Lord, discovering the joy that comes only from delighting in God's beauty, goodness, and love.

HOW TO PRAY
THIS BOOK

The purpose of this book is to open a gate for you, to make accessible the spiritual insight and wisdom of one of history's most extraordinary men, Augustine of Hippo.

This is not a book for mere reading. It invites you to meditate and pray its words on a daily basis over a period of thirty days and in a special way to enter into prayer through the unique doorway of Augustine's vibrant perspective on the restless soul's pursuit of God.

It is a handbook for a special kind of spiritual journey.

Before you read the "rules" for taking this journey, remember that this book is meant to free your spirit, not confine it. If on any day the meditation does not resonate well for you, turn elsewhere to find a passage which seems to best fit the spirit of your day and your soul. Don't hesitate to repeat a day as often as you like until you feel that you have discovered what the Spirit, through the words of the author, has to say to your spirit.

To help you along the way, here are some suggestions on one way to use this book as a cornerstone of your daily prayers. They are based on the three forms of prayer central to Western spiritual tradition: the lesson, the meditation, and the petition. The author of the classic *Cloud of Unknowing* has written that "they might better be called reading, reflecting, and praying. These three are so linked together that there can be no profitable reflection without first reading or hearing. Nor will beginners or even the spiritually adept come to true prayer without first taking time to reflect on what they have heard or read."

So for these thirty days there are readings for the beginning of the day that are developed from the writings of Augustine. There follows a meditation in the form of a mantra to carry with you for reflection throughout the day. And there is an exercise for bringing your day to an end that asks you to find a place of quiet dark where you might enter into silence as well as a final petitionary prayer at day's end.

But the forms and suggestions are not meant to become a straitjacket. Go where the Spirit leads you.

MY DAY BEGINS

As the day begins, set aside a quiet moment in a quiet place to do the reading provided for the day.

The passages are short; they never run more than a few hundred words. They have been carefully selected, though, to give a spiritual focus, a spiritual center to your whole day. They are designed to remind you, as another day begins, of your own existence at a spiritual level. They are meant to put you in the presence of the spiritual master who is your companion and teacher on this journey. The opening passages are framed as God's direct address to the reader, thus inviting you into God's presence to start your day in dialog with him.

Do not be discouraged if you do not fully understand the reading. Focus on your heart's response.

A word of advice: proceed slowly. Very slowly. The passages have been broken down into sense lines to help you do just this. Don't read to get to the end, but to savor each word, each phrase, each image. There is no predicting, no determining in advance, what short phrase, what word will trigger a response in your spirit. Give God a chance. After all, you are not reading these passages, you are *praying* them. You are establishing a mood of spiritual attentiveness for your whole day. What's the rush?

All Through the Day

Immediately following the day's reading you will find a single sentence, a meditation in the form of a mantra. This phrase is meant as a companion for your spirit as it moves through a busy day. Write it down on a 3" x 5" card or on the appropriate page of your daybook. Look at it as often as you can. Repeat it quietly to yourself, and go on your way.

It is not meant to stop you in your tracks or to distract you from responsibilities but simply, gently, to remind you of the presence of God and your desire to respond to his presence.

My Day Is Ending

This is a time for letting go of the day, for entering a world of imaginative prayer.

We suggest that you choose a quiet, dark place that you can return to each day at its ending. When you come to it, your first task is to quiet your spirit. Sit or kneel . . . whatever stills your soul. Breathe deeply. Inhale, exhale—slowly and deliberately, again and again, until you feel your body let go of its tension.

Now, using the least possible light, follow the evening exercise slowly, phrase by phrase, stopping as it suggests. If you find your mind arguing with it, analyzing it, trying to figure out its meanings and goals, don't be surprised. Simply start again by quieting your mind and freeing your imagination. Put behind you, as best you can, all that consciously or unconsciously stands between you and God.

This exercise is not meant to last more than a few minutes. End it when you are comfortable doing so. During this time, you are invited to turn to the familiarity of a prayer based on Augustine's own words. It is an act of trust and confidence, an entryway into peaceful sleep, a simple evening prayer that gathers together the spiritual character of the day that is now ending as it began—in the presence of God.

It is a time for summary and closure.

Invite God to embrace you with love and to protect you through the night.

Sleep well.

Some Other Ways to Use This Book

1. Use it any way your spirit suggests. As mentioned earlier, skip a passage that doesn't resonate for you on a given day, or repeat for a second day or even several days a passage whose richness speaks to you. The truths of a spiritual life are not absorbed in a day, or for that matter, in a lifetime. So take your time. Be patient with the Lord. Be patient with yourself.

2. Take two passages and/or their mantras—the more contrasting the better—and "bang" them together. Spend time discovering how their similarities or differences illumine your path.

3. Start a spiritual journal to record and deepen your experience of this thirty-day journey. Using either the mantra or another phrase from the reading that appeals to you, write a spiritual account of your day, a spiritual reflection. Create your own meditation.

4. Join millions who are seeking to deepen their spiritual life by joining with others to form a small group. More and more people are doing just this to support each other in their mutual quest. Meet

once a week, or at least every other week, to discuss and pray about one of the meditations. There are many books and guides available to help you make such a group effective.

John Kirvan, Series Editor

THIRTY DAYS WITH
AUGUSTINE OF HIPPO

DAY ONE

My Day Begins
God speaks . . .

I wish for you to know me, love me, and rejoice in me.
And, if you cannot do these perfectly in your earthly
life, fear not:
I invite you to advance to higher degrees every day,
until you can come closer to doing them in perfection.

Let the knowledge of me increase in you here,
that it may be full hereafter.
Let your love grow every day more and more here,
that it may be perfect hereafter;
that your joy may be full in me.

You know that I am a God of truth.
I make good gracious promises to you,
that your joy may be full;
to my honor and glory,
as the Father, the Son, and the Holy Spirit
I live and reign,
one God, now and forever.

ALL THROUGH THE DAY

Advance to higher degrees every day.

MY DAY IS ENDING

I RESPOND . . .

Watch, O Lord, with those who wake, or watch, or
weep tonight,
and give your angels charge over those who sleep.

As this day comes to a close, O God,
I know that I have not done my best—
to know you, love you, and rejoice in you
as you desire of me.
But I take comfort that you are perfect where I am not,
and that, despite my failures, your loving hand is
always there
to draw me closer through each hour of every day.

Teach me to be glad
that my time here is short,
that the hour that I come to know you more perfectly
draws near.
You have promised me that I can rest assured that this
is true,

because you are a God of truth.

Amen.

DAY TWO

MY DAY BEGINS

GOD SPEAKS . . .

O let my light,
my truth,
speak to the light of your heart,
not your own darkness.

You fall into sin,
and become dark;
but even then,
even then I love you.

You went astray, but I remembered you.
You heard my voice behind you,
calling you to return,
but scarcely heard it,
through the raging of the enemies of peace.

See now,
you return in distress and pant after my fountain.
Let no one forbid you!
You will drink of this and live.
Do not regard your life as your own.

18

For you have lived ill.

You were death to yourself,
but I revive you.
I speak to you,
do you speak with me?

A ʟʟ T ʜ ʀ ᴏ ᴜ ɢ ʜ ᴛ ʜ ᴇ D ᴀ ʏ

Do not regard your life as your own.

M ʏ D ᴀ ʏ I s E ɴ ᴅ ɪ ɴ ɢ

I ʀᴇsᴘᴏɴᴅ . . ..

Watch, O Lord, with those who wake, or watch, or
weep tonight,
and give your angels charge over those who sleep.

Do not let the light of my heart grow as dark
as the night that draws near.
Even when I go astray, I know that you will never
forsake me.

I know that you will call to me and
remind me to listen and heed your voice.
I know that you will remind me of your love,
and that my life is not my own.

I will always return to you, O God,
and die to sin and revive in you.
Let no enemy stand in my way
as I journey back to you.
Amen.

DAY THREE

···

M Y D A Y B E G I N S

G OD SPEAKS . . .

I pour out my grace,
and descend plentifully into your heart.
I enlighten the dark corners of this neglected dwelling,
and, there, I scatter cheerful beams of light.

I dwell in the soul that longs to be my temple.
I water the barren soil, overrun with weeds and briars,
and lost for lack of cultivating,
and I make it fruitful with dew from heaven.

I come with refreshment
for those who languish and faint.
I guide those who sail in the tempestuous sea of the
world. I am the only haven of the shipwrecked.
I come in glory as the crown of the living and the
safeguard of the dying.
I come with great mercy and make you fit to receive
my grace.

A LL T HROUGH THE D AY

Make me fit to receive God's grace.

MY DAY IS ENDING

I RESPOND . . .

Watch, O Lord, with those who wake, or watch, or
weep tonight,
and give your angels charge over those who sleep.

O Lord, teach me to tend to the fields of my heart.
You've given me an excess of all that I need to flourish
and grow.
You have planted seeds of grace, watered with love,
and provided sunlight through your glory.

Despite this, my harvest is often barren because
I have squandered your gifts or failed to use them as
you have asked me.
Yet, in your mercy, I do not go without.
O God, you always provide.

Through this day, give me courage to not give up—
even when I feel as though I have been shipwrecked in
my faith.
Renew my strength and make me fit to glorify you
through my labors in this life.
Amen.

DAY FOUR

....

God speaks . . .

O how do you call on me, your God and Lord,
since when you call for me,
you are calling me into yourself?
What room have you made there within you,
where I, who made heaven and earth,
can come into you?

Do heaven and earth, which I have made,
and in which I have made you, contain me?
Nothing which exists could exist without me,
so whatever does exist contains me.

Since you too exist,
why do you seek to know if I am also in you?
You would not be if I were not in you.
I am found in all things: the heavens, the earth,
and you.

Though you are broken through sin,
do not think I have been poured out.

I am not dismayed, I will uplift you.
I am not scattered, I will gather you.

All Through the Day

Whatever exists contains God.

My Day Is Ending

I respond . . .

Watch, O Lord, with those who wake, or watch, or
weep tonight,
and give your angels charge over those who sleep.

O God, I know that I am fearfully and
wonderfully made.
All of creation declares and sings of your glory.
In spite of this, I sometimes doubt that your goodness
is within me
because I have filled my heart with things
other than you.

Never cease to remind me that you are in all things—
even me.
When I fail to see this because of the darkness of sin,
help me know that hell has not won.
Your love abounds, you have not abandoned me.

I yearn to make room for you, my God,
so that I can recognize you clearly
when I search inside myself.
Declutter my heart, Lord.
I want to fill the empty spaces with you.

DAY FIVE

My Day Begins

God speaks . . .

Ask not of me
silver and gold,
honor and glory,
nor the pleasures of the world.

Instead, I grant you grace to seek my kingdom,
my righteousness,
and give you what you need for body and life.
I behold your desire to know me.
This is pleasing in my sight.

I hear your petition through Jesus Christ,
who is at my right hand, mediator and advocate,
through whom I sought you that you might seek me;
my Word, through whom I made you and all things.
My only Son, through whom I call you to adoption,
who intercedes for you,
and in whom are hidden all the treasures of wisdom
and knowledge.

All Through the Day

In Christ, all treasures of wisdom and knowledge
are hidden.

My Day Is Ending

I respond . . .

Watch, O Lord, with those who wake, or watch, or
weep tonight,
and give your angels charge over those who sleep.

O Lord, Jesus Christ, I am often tempted by things of
this world.
I find in myself the desire for money, power,
and pleasure.
I know that these things do not glorify you, my God.
Come to my aid and teach me to pursue you instead.

I know that where you are found,
I will find righteousness, truth, hope, wisdom, and my
daily bread.
There is nothing more that I could need,
so help to rearrange my heart and leave room
for only you.
I hope to carry each cross that I am given,
but know that I will not always carry them well.

When you see me struggle,
give me the patience to persevere.
I know this will take the course of my entire life,
but I am willing.

DAY SIX

My Day Begins

God speaks . . .

I am the Lord, I am your Savior,
I have warned you that
I will require much
of those to whom I give much.

I will that all who have so great a heritage in me,
as you do,
will strive together more abundantly
to extend to others
what has been so richly enjoyed.

As you support the labors of others,
through your work and sweat alongside of them,
perhaps, in turn, they will support you in your work,
in bringing about the
fulfillment of my holy will.

All Through the Day

Extend to others what you have so richly enjoyed.

MY DAY IS ENDING

I RESPOND . . .

Watch, O Lord, with those who wake, or watch, or
weep tonight,
and give your angels charge over those who sleep.

Lord, I want to do your work.
I want those around me to know of your love like I do.
You have given so much,
but I feel I have returned so little,
and I often don't know where to start.

I desire to have the words to inflame other's hearts,
but, when I don't, help me to imitate you through all
that I do.
Perhaps, then, through my labors, they will come to
see you
through your love radiating so brilliantly out of me.

But, Lord, keep me humble.
Never fail to remind me of the source of the goodness
that flows forth from me,
for it is Christ alone who strengthens me and leads me
to victory.

DAY SEVEN

....

My Day Begins

God speaks . . .

Know that I am your God,
I am full of compassion.
When you commit and commend yourself to me,
I am in you and I give you life
and I help you to know me.

I am the goal of your long, earthly pilgrimage.
I am also your rest along the way,
so let your soul take refuge.
I will disperse the crowding turmoil
of worldly thoughts,
if you will only take shelter beneath the safety of
my wings.

I will let your heart and I will let your mind,
both raging seas filled with restless and constant waves,
find peace and solace in my presence.
Trust that the tempest will subside. I will bring you to
safer shores.

ALL THROUGH THE DAY

Find peace and solace in me.

MY DAY IS ENDING

I RESPOND . . .

Watch, O Lord, with those who wake, or watch, or
weep tonight,
and give your angels charge over those who sleep.

Lord, I am often overwhelmed.
Between painful anxieties over the future and bitter
regrets over the past,
I cannot see you here and now.
In these difficult moments, clear away the blindness in
me so that I may see.

When I grow weary, I will pause and rest in you.
I know that you comfort the afflicted and
give them strength.
I know that in your goodness, you will always provide.
Reach into me. Instill holy indifference to the things I
cannot control.

Help me to hear your voice calling out in
moments of strife,

instead of succumbing to the noise of temptation,
darkness, and sin,
because these things are but houses built upon
shifting sands.
My God, you are my firm foundation, my steadiness,
my path.

DAY EIGHT

....

G O D S P E A K S . . .

I Am Who Am.
I bountifully give all who seek me good gifts.
I give those who are weary their refreshment and food.
I gather your distracted thoughts and bring them into
harmony again.

I set prisoners free.
I stand at your door and knock.
Open it to me and I will enter
and I will set fire to the kindling in you.

I am the wellspring of life.
I am the light of eternal brightness.
I am where the just live.
All will be according to my word.

A L L T H R O U G H T H E D A Y

Open your door to my knock.

My Day Is Ending

I respond . . .

Watch, O Lord, with those who wake, or watch, or
weep tonight,
and give your angels charge over those who sleep.

Gracious God, I love the world that you have created
for me to live in.
I can't help but see you in everything around me;
everything that is true, good, and beautiful.
Truly, your creation speaks of you in joyful tongues
that all can understand.

But, at times, events show me that this world is not
my home
and I begin to feel that I am a prisoner
to darkness and sin.
My soul becomes sorrowful and I fear my weeping may
never end.
I ache for my citizenship in heaven.

But until then, Lord, remind me that these moments
are not without meaning.
I must be patient. Wherever there is darkness, light
abounds all the more.

Just as your suffering on the cross opened
the gates of heaven,
the sorrows that each day may bring can make holiness
reign in me.
Amen.

.

DAY NINE

My Day Begins

God speaks . . .

I am God your Father,
I will always invite you to pray.
Be glad of this because I will grant what you ask
when you ask something of me that is according to
my will.

I hear you even when you tremble in darkness.
Stretch forth your hand to me and I will grasp it.
I will shine your light before you and, soon,
you will be recalled from your wanderings.

I am your perfect guide.
I will never lead you astray, but, if you stumble,
I will always unite you with me again
for I have restored you through Jesus Christ.

All Through the Day

I hear you even when you tremble in darkness.

MY DAY IS ENDING

I RESPOND . . .

Watch, O Lord, with those who wake, or watch, or
weep tonight,
and give your angels charge over those who sleep.

My God, I have beseeched you for many things.
In your love for me,
you have granted so many of my requests.
Forgive me when I've been ungrateful for the gifts
you've given me today.
Forgive me when I've focused on the prayers that
went unanswered.

I know that you always hear me, but
I realize that I do not always ask what you will for me.
Teach me to accept that I do not always know best.
I know you will lead me kindly, Lord, to where you
want me to be.

Fill me with the courage to continue my journey
to you.
I know your glory and goodness
will light the path ahead.

Even when I stray and travel
down crooked,
winding roads,
always find me and make me whole.
Amen.

DAY TEN

My Day Begins

God speaks . . .

Many of my attributes are unspeakable,
but know that I am holy and mighty and
that my power and wisdom have no end.
Before me all earthly powers will tremble.

Know that I am love;
I am your Father.
I desire for you to love and worship me.
Know that I will console you always.

I will shine forth rays of my light into your mind.
I will always guide you into my perfect light.
If you accept it, I will illumine you.

All darkness will flee if you let the holy flames
of my all-encompassing love burn in your heart.
It will make it pure, so that you can see.
It is the pure in heart who will rest in me.

I have set you free.
I have drawn you to me, so don't forsake me.

Instead, take comfort always in my grace.
Allow me to guide, rule, and perfect you
for my kingdom.

All Through the Day

I will always guide you into my perfect light.

My Day Is Ending

I respond . . .

Watch, O Lord, with those who wake, or watch, or
weep tonight,
and give your angels charge over those who sleep.

Almighty God, at the end of this day, I am before you
in awe;
in awe of your vast goodness, glory, might, and,
most of all,
your desire to know me and love me—
despite all my faults, failures, and imperfections.

Nothing can compare to you.
I know that my mind will never fully grasp you, and
that I will always carry doubt,
but I will try to not let this distress me because

I know you are there because your love for me burns
brilliantly for all to see.

Instruct me to respond to the promptings of your grace
by allowing it to shape my heart, order my desires, and
soothe my uncertainties.
Mold my entire being, Lord.
I want to come into your kingdom.
Amen.

DAY ELEVEN

··

My Day Begins

God speaks . . .

You know, as my creation,
that you've often acknowledged yourself
as altogether unworthy of my love.
But be assured that I do love you.

You think that you are not good enough to serve me,
but know that I just ask that you offer me the best
service you can.
I have imparted to you my own excellence.
Let this supply you to overcome your perceived
lack of worth.

I will help you cease from sins against my will.
I will enable you to guard and govern yourself to begin
and finish your course,
that when the race of life has been run,
you may sleep in peace and rest in me.

I will be with you to the end.
I will ensure that your final sleep may be
true rest indeed,

that this rest has perfect security,
and in that security, a blessed eternity.

ALL THROUGH THE DAY

I will be with you to the end.

MY DAY IS ENDING

I RESPOND . . .

Watch, O Lord, with those who wake, or watch, or
weep tonight,
and give your angels charge over those who sleep.

Most Holy God, you made me in your image.
You gave me my soul, my will, and my intellect.
You looked upon these things
and said that they were good,
yet, at times, I struggle to recognize this in myself.

It is harder to see my worth when I have drifted from
the course you've willed
and when I have been slow to return to your embrace.
You know what is best for me
and what will preserve me.
Protect me and help me to stay steady in my course.

And, as I find myself growing weary as I prepare to rest
this night,
remind me of my final resting place.
I can never know which night will be my last, but
I am prepared to enter into it joyfully.
Amen.

DAY TWELVE

MY DAY BEGINS

GOD SPEAKS . . .

Blessed are all my saints,
I have been their God and King,
as they have travelled over the tempestuous
sea of mortality,
and have at last made the desired port of
peace and happiness.
I will be gracious to you who are still on your
dangerous voyage.

I remember and help those in distress,
I remember those who are exposed
to the rough storms of troubles and temptations.
I will strengthen your weaknesses,
that you may fight valiantly in the spiritual war that
rages around you.

I will help you fight against your own
negligence and cowardice,
I will defend you from the treachery of your
unfaithful hearts.

I am the Lord and I grant that your vessel will be
brought safely to shore
to your desired haven.

All Through the Day

I remember those who are exposed to the rough storms
of troubles and temptations.

My Day Is Ending

I respond . . .

Watch, O Lord, with those who wake, or watch, or
weep tonight,
and give your angels charge over those who sleep.

Ruler of heaven and earth,
I desire nothing more but to enter
your heavenly kingdom.
I yearn to praise you there, worship you there, and
know you there.
I want to know the happiness that only you
can provide.

Lord, allow me to parade alongside all your
saints and angels
so that I may joyously unite my songs of praise
with theirs.

Help me to nourish this desire each day
because I am weak and the pleasures of this world
distract me.

The road to heaven is always lined with many dangers.
With your aid, my sins, temptations, and faults will be
only temporary obstacles and this body, this humble,
mortal vessel, will arrive safely at your shores.
I know you will quench my thirst, heal my wounds,
and celebrate with me the victory that has already been
won by your Son, Jesus Christ.

Amen.

DAY THIRTEEN

....

M Y D A Y B E G I N S

G OD SPEAKS . . .

I look on you, my people,
and make vanish all the darkness of your souls
with radiant beams of my brightness.
They will fill you with holy love,
and I will open you to the treasures of my wisdom.

Your desires are known to me,
and I will complete what I have begun—
what my Spirit has awakened in you
to ask of me in prayer.

You seek my face,
so I will turn to you and show you my glory.
Then your longings will be satisfied
and the peace you seek shall be perfected.

A LL T H R O U G H T H E D A Y

I will complete what I have begun.

M Y D A Y I S E N D I N G

I RESPOND . . .

Watch, O Lord, with those who wake, or watch, or
weep tonight,
and give your angels charge over those who sleep.

Good and gracious God, you are a merciful ruler.
Your work in me is not yet complete and my
transgressions are many,
but you still govern my life with an abundance of
mercy and justice.
Help me to be grateful for this gift that I do not
deserve. I am so undeserving.

When darkness and sin surround me,
banish them from my life and smile upon me
once again.
I beseech you for the grace and the light not to stumble
again, to see clearly the path I must follow, and for the
strength to always turn to you in prayer.

And, when I struggle with what I discover there,
help me to trust that you have chosen well for me and
that your stirrings within me only lead to peace.
Guide me, Lord, through no challenge that would not
lead me closer to you.
Amen.

DAY FOURTEEN

GOD SPEAKS . . .

I am the light of the blind and the strength of the weak.
I am the light of those who see and I am the strength of
the strong;
I listen to your soul. I hear your prayers.
I hear you crying out from the depths.

I am the Lord. I help you to turn and seek me.
I will never forsake my creatures even when you have
forsaken me.
Turn and seek me. You know I will reside
in your hearts
when you confess to me and weep at my feet.

I will gently wipe away your tears,
and you will weep more, but for joy;
because I, the Lord who made you,
have remade you and comforted you.

ALL THROUGH THE DAY

I hear you crying out.

My Day Is Ending

I RESPOND . . .

Watch, O Lord, with those who wake, or watch, or
weep tonight,
and give your angels charge over those who sleep.

My God, I know that you have said that you will
always forgive,
but, when I have done wrong,
I often become despondent.
I am too afraid or too prideful to ask for your mercy;
I feel that I am not deserving and I turn
further from you.

Do not let me forsake you, O God.
Even when covered in darkness, I know that you hear
my cries.
Allow your light to pierce through these shadows,
and rescue me from a fate
that you do not desire for me.

I will confess all my sins to you and I will seek reform.
Deliver me from the desire to weep for sins that have
already been forgiven.
Instead, I will rejoice because I have heard you
and you have called me into you once again.
Amen.

DAY FIFTEEN

My Day Begins

God speaks . . .

I am the blessed Lord Jesus Christ,
I ask you to thank me for the boundless love
I give to you.
I have redeemed the human race
by my precious death on the Cross.

I shed my blood for you,
a poor sinner.
I feed your soul with my Body,
and I quicken your spirit with my Blood.

You always grow in the knowledge of me,
in awe and love, in how you live your life,
and in abiding as a true member of my Body,
the holy Catholic Church.

All Through the Day

I shed my blood for you.

MY DAY IS ENDING

I RESPOND . . .

Watch, O Lord, with those who wake, or watch, or
weep tonight,
and give your angels charge over those who sleep.

Christ Jesus, you are the perfect sacrifice.
I know that without you, I could never enter the
kingdom of heaven.
Abide in me in greater and greater quantities,
so that I may die to myself daily and become
more like you.

Make me worthy to receive your Body and Blood;
My own actions alone could never merit such a gift.
Only then, through your sacrificial love,
can I truly live,
only then, guided by your Spirit, can I carry out the
mission you've entrusted to me.

Give me the words to speak of your goodness,
I want to bring others to your compassionate heart.
Gather us all under your banner, Lord Jesus,
our souls cry out to be united with you.
Amen.

DAY SIXTEEN

My Day Begins

God speaks . . .

I am God the Holy Spirit,
I am of one essence with the Father and the Son,
and I proceed forth from them.
Together, we are all in all—love, lover, and beloved.

I descended on the Lord Jesus Christ
in the form of a dove,
and I descended on his disciples and inspired them as
tongues of flame.
I wish to descend and abide in you as well.
As I do, I will ask you to pray that I chase
from your soul
all the darkness of evil and release each of your
attachments to sin.

I will kindle in you the abundant, cleansing light of
my grace
and the zealous fires of my all-encompassing love.
Through this, I will live and reign in you,
as true God, forever and ever.

ALL THROUGH THE DAY

Pray that I chase from your soul all the darkness
of evil.

MY DAY IS ENDING

I RESPOND . . .

Watch, O Lord, with those who wake, or watch, or
weep tonight,
and give your angels charge over those who sleep.

O Holy Spirit, the Paraclete, ignite my mortal heart.
Quicken it to desire the eternal dance that is found
only in union with you.
Teach it to give fully, wholly, and unselfishly,
as you do, because
I know that, with you as my guide, my cup could never
run dry.

Descend on me as you descended upon Jesus.
Descend on me as you descended upon the apostles.
I will create for you a room in my heart
and beseech you to drive out all evil
that may reside there.

I ask you to teach me how to pray,
Breath of the Almighty.

I want to speak the words that will lead me closest to
your will.
I will walk closer and closer to the fires of your
divine love,
knowing that this path will lead to your eternal reign
in me.
Amen.

DAY SEVENTEEN

My Day Begins

God speaks . . .

I am the Lord. I am your God.
I will lead you and guide you to find hope under the
shadow of my wings.
I will support you when you are small and helpless.
I will support you when your movements grow slow
and your hair becomes gray.

When your strength is from me,
it is true strength.
When you rely upon your own,
understand that it is only weakness.

Return to me, my people, that your weary souls may
rise toward me,
rise past all things that I have created,
and reach out to me. I have wonderfully made you and
with me lies your refreshment, comfort,
and true strength.

ALL THROUGH THE DAY

I will always support you.

MY DAY IS ENDING

I RESPOND . . .

Watch, O Lord, with those who wake, or watch, or
weep tonight,
and give your angels charge over those who sleep.

My God, be with me each and every day of my life.
As you protected me as an infant, I know you protect
me now.
Help me to be unafraid as my body continues to age,
I know that my time here is limited. I know that my
time grows short.

But, as my earthly strength fades, grant me your peace.
I desire to accept that this world is not my home
and that
my true strength is not in this body, nor in this mind,
but, instead, is only found in you.

With your strength, I will inherit
the kingdom of heaven.
I know this because my soul yearns to return to the
place it was made,

it seeks shelter and refreshment in your shadow.
Lord, give me hope and ensure that I will know true
and eternal happiness.

Amen.

DAY EIGHTEEN

MY DAY BEGINS

GOD SPEAKS . . .

I, the Almighty God,
care for you as if I thought of you alone,
but I care for all as if each of you were one.

You see the things of the earth pass away,
and you watch events come and go,
but I will be constant. I will remain forever.

I, your God and Father,
have entrusted to you all that you have received
from me,
because then, you can lose nothing.

I, the Lord,
have made you for myself, and your heart
will find no rest,
until it rests in me.

ALL THROUGH THE DAY

Your heart will find no rest until it rests in me.

M Y D AY I S E NDING

Watch, O Lord, with those who wake, or watch, or
weep tonight,
and give your angels charge over those who sleep.

Loving Father, your creative power knows no bounds.
Your people are as numerous as the stars,
yet you love each of us as if we were the only light
found in your sky.
Truly, you are a good and gracious shepherd.

So permit me to not be distressed at the state
of the world.
Deliver me from the belief that goodness has been
vanquished from it
for I know that sin and death are but
temporary afflictions.
Evil will not triumph. I know that you alone
can reign forever.

All that I have is yours, O God,
even the breath found in my lungs and the blood that
flows in my veins.
Even the beats of my heart belong not to me,

so prepare me, as I prepare to rest; to one day return
these gifts to you.

Amen.

DAY NINETEEN

MY DAY BEGINS

GOD SPEAKS . . .

I am the Lord, your God,
I am your one hope, so hear me;
be not unwilling, through your weariness, to seek me,
but, instead, always ardently seek my face.

I will give you the strength to seek,
since I have made you in order to find me,
and I have given you the hope of finding me
more and more.
May you always remember me, understand me, and
love me.

Your strengths and your weaknesses are known to me:
I will preserve one and heal the other.
Your knowledge and your ignorance are known to me:
Where I have opened to you, I will receive you
as you enter;
where I have closed to you, I will open to you
as you knock.

All Through the Day

I am your one hope.

My Day Is Ending

I respond . . .

Watch, O Lord, with those who wake, or watch, or
weep tonight,
and give your angels charge over those who sleep.

O God, I present myself before you in weariness—
not just in body from the efforts of this day,
but also in spirit.
It often appears easier to seek shelter from my woes in
worldly things;
make good your promise to give me the strength to
seek you instead.

I am created to pursue you with my whole being.
I was designed by you to be holy.
But I am flawed and my actions do not always reflect
this reality.
Surpass my imperfection so that I may
reach out to you unhindered.

I know that this is your will for me, loving God.

It was you who prompted me to cry out in prayer.

You know that my spirit thirsts; you know what most
I need.

Never let me forget that you are the wellspring of
my refreshment.

Amen.

DAY TWENTY

My Day Begins

God speaks . . .

I am God. I am the merciful Father.
I ask you to remember and exclaim the mercies
that I have given to you throughout your life.
I wish to drench you with my love.

It will soak your skin and settle deep into your bones
until they cry out in awe to me,
"Who is like you, O Lord?"

I have broken your bonds,
and, for this, I ask you to offer me your thanks.
Declare to all how I have broken them.

When all who worship me hear you, they shall say,
"Blessed be the Lord, in heaven and on earth,
great and wonderful is his name."

All Through the Day

Who is like you, O Lord?

MY DAY IS ENDING

I RESPOND . . .

Watch, O Lord, with those who wake, or watch, or
weep tonight,
and give your angels charge over those who sleep.

O God of Mercy, your great compassion knows
no bounds.
Seventy times seven times have I transgressed
against you,
and seventy times seven times you have forgiven me
and allowed your love and grace to abound in me all
the more.

There are none like you, O Lord.
All of creation is humbled before you.
It proclaims your glory to me and makes you known to
all as the maker of all that is good.

Increase your presence in me
so that I may do the same.
I wish for others to recognize your goodness
through my exclamations of your great blessings, glory,
and love.
I wish for others to tremble in awe at your name.
Amen.

DAY TWENTY-ONE

MY DAY BEGINS

GOD SPEAKS . . .

Late have you loved me,
my beauty so ancient and so new,
late have you loved me!

Behold, I was within you,
but you were outside, seeking there for me
among the shapely things I have made;
to these, instead, you rushed headlong.

I was with you but you were not with me.
Worldly things held you back far from me,
those things which would have no being
were they not in me.
I called, shouted, broke through your deafness;
I flared, blazed, banished your blindness;
You gasped, and now you pant for me;
You tasted, and now you hunger and thirst;
I have touched you, and now you burn for my peace.

ALL THROUGH THE DAY

I have always been within you.

MY DAY IS ENDING

I RESPOND . . .

Watch, O Lord, with those who wake, or watch, or
weep tonight,
and give your angels charge over those who sleep.

Eternal God, late have I loved you.
I have often not realized that I was seeking and
desiring you
when I have tried to fill the void in me
with things that are not of you.

You have always resided deep within me,
but I have not always recognized you there
because my senses were clouded by my sins.
Forgive me, O Lord, for my past sins—even those I
have committed today.

Never allow me to fall into deafness again.
Always break through my ignorance and
inflame my being;

rouse me from my slumbers with your love
and your light
so that I may rise tomorrow and devote all of my labors
to pursuing you.
Amen.

DAY TWENTY-TWO

MY DAY BEGINS

GOD SPEAKS . . .

I am the light of every heart that sees me,
the life of every soul that loves me,
the strength of every mind that seeks me.

I will help you to be steadfast in your love.
I will be the joy of your heart;
I take it all to myself and allow it to remain there.

The house of your soul is narrow;
I will enlarge it so that I may enter.
Where it is ruinous, I will repair it.

Confess your sins to me and I shall cleanse you,
I will cleanse you of even your most secret faults,
and I will spare you, since you are my servant, from
strange sins.

ALL THROUGH THE DAY

I will be the joy of your heart.

My Day Is Ending

I respond . . .

Watch, O Lord, with those who wake, or watch, or
weep tonight,
and give your angels charge over those who sleep.

My radiant Lord, you illumine all who draw near.
My heart has been pierced so thoroughly by your joy
that I cannot help but to traverse deeper
into your mystery.
Give me the strength to overcome any obstacles
on my journey.

My understandings are but a bucket of water amidst
an ocean,
but, through your graces, I will never cease my bailing,
because even one step closer to you, O Lord,
is a step that is well worth taking.

But, as I near ever closer to the end of my race,
heal me of the wounds that I have imposed on myself
through stumbling.
Allow my gaze to grow fixated on you,
and may my path grow ever straighter.
Amen.

DAY TWENTY-THREE

....

G OD SPEAKS . . .

I am the Lord, your God.
I am most merciful,
most secret, most present,
most constant, yet able to change all things.

I am never new, yet I am never old.
I am always in action, yet am always quiet.
I create, uphold, and perfect.

Who has anything but what I have given to them?
What can anyone say of me when they speak?
I will have mercy on you
that you may speak of me and praise me.

A LL T HROUGH THE D AY

I will have mercy on you.

My Day Is Ending

I respond . . .

Watch, O Lord, with those who wake, or watch, or
weep tonight,
and give your angels charge over those who sleep.

God, most loving, you hold me into being each day.
Through this, I know that you love me and
that you are constantly present to me.
Despite this, I understand so little
of who you really are.

Yet, I believe I could speak volumes about you,
and could sing your praises forever,
so never cease to give me the words that you most
want to hear
from my lips when I come to you in prayer.

All that is good in my life has come from you,
most especially the gifts of forgiveness and mercy.
None can give gifts as good as these, O Lord,
so I can be patient and gracious until I can know you
more fully.
Amen.

DAY TWENTY-FOUR

MY DAY BEGINS

GOD SPEAKS . . .

I will watch over you, as your Lord.
I will watch with those who wake, or watch, or weep.
I will give the angels charge over those who sleep.
I will tend to the sick ones.

I will rest all the weary ones.
I will bless the dying ones
and soothe the suffering ones.
I will pity the afflicted ones and shield the joyous ones.
And all for the sake of my love for you.

ALL THROUGH THE DAY

I will watch over you.

MY DAY IS ENDING

I RESPOND . . .

Watch, O Lord, with those who wake, or watch, or
weep tonight,
and give your angels charge over those who sleep.

Your reign knows no bounds, O Lord.
You are a most just and kind ruler
over all your creation,
so I know my words will not fall silent upon your ears
when I beseech you: Don't let your people fall
into disarray.

I want to be your humble servant,
I know that you watch over me as I live even when I
make mistakes.
You know that through my labors my body
will grow weary,
so I will need your help, O Lord, so that I don't just
rot away.

Your angels standing guard each night at my bedside,
so I will never be alone if temptation should arrive.
This is a constant witness of your loving care,
so never let me forget that the battle
has already been won.
Amen.

DAY TWENTY-FIVE

GOD SPEAKS . . .

I am the Lord; I will hear your prayer;
I will not let your soul faint under my discipline,
nor let you faint in confessing
to others all the mercies I have provided.

I have drawn you out of your most evil ways,
that you might become a delight to me above all things,
that, free from sin, you may most entirely love me.
I will clasp your hand with all of my affections.

I will rescue you from every temptation,
even until your very last day.
Behold, I am the Lord, your King and your God.
In my mercy, you will always be forgiven.

ALL THROUGH THE DAY

I will clasp your hand with all of my affections.

MY DAY IS ENDING

I RESPOND . . .

Watch, O Lord, with those who wake, or watch, or
weep tonight,
and give your angels charge over those who sleep.

Christ, my king and Savior, never cease to draw me out
of the abyss.
I want to follow your statutes and keep
your commandments,
for you have told me that they will quench my thirst
for all eternity
and allow me to journey to the full potential of who
you created me to be.

I am comforted that you delight in me,
and want to experience the joy of my heavenly Father's
love, always.
So never hesitate to guide and correct me, O God;
I want to break free from the shackles of temptation.

But, when I fail to rise to the occasion,
drench my entire being with your graces so that
I can scale any obstacle to seeking your forgiveness
and proclaim aloud your mercies for all to hear.
Amen.

DAY TWENTY-SIX

MY DAY BEGINS

GOD SPEAKS . . .

I am the Lord,
I am the light, the way, the truth, the life;
In me, there is no darkness, error, vanity, or death.

I am the light without darkness;
the way without wandering.
I am the truth without error;
I am life without death.

I, the Lord, said, "Let there be light,"
and I saw light eschew the darkness.
I will ensure that you see the way
and avoid wandering.
You shall see the truth and shun error.

You shall see life and escape death:
I will illuminate your blind soul sitting in darkness
and death.
I will direct your feet to follow the way of peace.

ALL THROUGH THE DAY

You shall see life and escape death.

My Day Is Ending

I respond . . .

Watch, O Lord, with those who wake, or watch, or
weep tonight,
and give your angels charge over those who sleep.

O Light of the World, your glory knows no bounds.
I know you find all people that are searching for you,
just as you once found me and sent me forth along
your way;
the way of light, truth, and eternal life.

Your way will preserve me from error,
instill in me a love for truth,
and allow me to escape forever
from the darkness of death.
Grant me the strength to never stray from this path.

Because, as I travel down it, scales fall from my eyes,
But I have long to go and, if I were to see you now,
surely I would be blinded.
Prepare me each day so that one day I may look upon
your face
and, at long last, rest in your peace forever.
Amen.

DAY TWENTY-SEVEN

MY DAY BEGINS

GOD SPEAKS . . .

I want to know and love you,
so that you may find happiness in me.
Since you cannot fully achieve this on earth,
I will help you improve
until the day you may do so fully.

I will enable you to know me ever more on earth,
so that you may know me perfectly in heaven.
In following my way, your joy may be great on earth
and perfect in heaven.
I will keep my promises and grant you this so that your
joy may be full.

Before this time arrives, let your mind dwell
on that happiness.
Let your tongue speak of it, your heart pine for it, your
mouth exclaim it,
your soul hunger for it, your flesh thirst for it, and your
entire being desire it
until you enter into eternal joy forever.

All Through the Day

Let your entire being desire God.

My Day Is Ending

I respond . . .

Watch, O Lord, with those who wake, or watch, or
weep tonight,
and give your angels charge over those who sleep.

Eternal God, purify the recesses of my intellect,
for I know that it is a gracious gift
that bears your image,
but I have filled it with things of this world and
attachment to sin
instead of the happiness and wisdom that come with
love of you.

Grant me your grace and guide me each day, O Lord,
through bringing me to people, places, and encounters
that will help me to grow in my understandings of you.
This will restore my intellect and plant the seeds of
unquenchable desire.

Soon, I will think of naught but you and your
holy kingdom.

Already, my heart grows weary of having only tastes of
your goodness.

Hungering and thirsting, it cries out for more and more
each day.

Holy God, deliver me from these pangs of absence. I
want to be filled with your joy.

Amen.

DAY TWENTY-EIGHT

My Day Begins

God speaks . . .

I want you to know me and desire only me.
I want you to do everything for the sake of me.
Humble yourself and exalt me,
think of nothing but me.

I will let you die to yourself and live forever in me.
If you trust in me, you will become indifferent to
whatever happens.
Banish your selfishness, and desire
to follow me forever.
Fly from yourself. Take refuge in me.
I will defend you.

I want you to be among those who inherit my kingdom.
Put your trust in me, not yourself.
Be willing to obey me.
Cling to nothing but me. Be unafraid to be poor
because of me.
Look upon me, love me, call upon me.

ALL THROUGH THE DAY

Become indifferent to whatever happens
and trust in me.

MY DAY IS ENDING

I RESPOND . . .

Watch, O Lord, with those who wake, or watch, or
weep tonight,
and give your angels charge over those who sleep.

My God, this world is full of distraction.
Even as I pray tonight, I am in danger of succumbing
to it;
worries and thoughts of many other things swirl about.
Assist me in obtaining your silence, your comfort, and
your peace.

I offer to you my trepidations, my doubts,
and my selfishness.
Wither these faults and insecurities found inside me;
rain your grace and mercy upon my soul.
Allow a new life—rooted in you—to spring
forth vibrantly.

Intertwine the sickly branches and vines of my will
with your own.

Make them healthy, whole, confident, and strong.
Only then, basking in the warmth of your glory, may I
grow to new heights,
be liberated from all anxiety, and find rest in the
kingdom of heaven.
Amen.

DAY TWENTY-NINE

MY DAY BEGINS

GOD SPEAKS . . .

Sing to me a new song and
strip away your old self.
You know that the new does not belong with the old.
Only the new can sing of me;
they have known my graces.

Let your love for me breathe with newness,
It will ensure that it echoes throughout the songs that
you sing,
but I speak not of song that springs forth from
your tongue.
Rather, I speak of that which comes from your life.

Be always searching for the way to sing to me.
Sing beautifully, but without searching for words
and lyrics.
Instead, always be jubilant. What is sung inside cannot
be spelled out in words.
Allow your heart to birth what cannot be spoken.

All Through the Day

Always be jubilant.

My Day Is Ending

I respond . . .

Watch, O Lord, with those who wake, or watch, or
weep tonight,
and give your angels charge over those who sleep.

My God, my soul is bursting with your music.
Your grace resounded powerfully and sweetly
in the depths.
This quickened me; I can no longer remain still
or silent.
I must sing your praises always.

I must follow the steps you have laid before me,
without listing or careening about.
If each step that lays true becomes a joyful noise,
accompany my steps, O God,
until they swell into a symphony.

Let the choices that I make each day
speak loudly of the love that I have for you.

With your joy residing inside me,
I can never grow silent.
May your glory echo throughout the ages forever.
Amen.

DAY THIRTY

••

My Day Begins

God speaks . . .

I will show you how to resist the proud.
I will give grace to the humble.
I will guide you to your innermost parts
and allow you to see my immutable light with the eye
of your soul.

This is the light that has made you.
I am eternal truth, true love, and beloved eternity.
You are not yet ready for vision of me,
but you have heard me from afar and there is no
reason for doubt.

Marvel upon me and love me.
By the natural weight of your fallen will,
I know you will not stand still
in the enjoyment of me, but
I have snatched you up by my glory and my memory
will remain in you forever.

ALL THROUGH THE DAY

I am eternal truth, true love, and beloved eternity.

MY DAY IS ENDING

I RESPOND . . .

Watch, O Lord, with those who wake, or watch, or
weep tonight,
and give your angels charge over those who sleep.

Beloved Lord, I will always need your assistance in
defending me from my own pride,
in teaching me humility,
and in sweeping away the dark clouds of my soul
that my sins have allowed to accumulate each and
every day.

I know that your light can pierce this darkness,
so ready me to receive it and be open to it.
For, despite my deafness, I have still heard you calling
in the distance
and I know that the time of my demise will shortly be
at hand.

Do not let me forget you, O God,
even when I, in my brokenness, have tried to run far
from you.

You are the only source and spring of happiness
and truth;
I cannot live this life, or the next, without you.
Amen.

ONE FINAL WORD

This book is no more than a gateway—a gateway to the spiritual experience and wisdom of a specific teacher that opens on your own spiritual path. It is an opportunity to join the dialogue between Augustine and God.

Now it is time to join Augustine in some final words of worship for the God whose beauty captured Augustine's heart—and has, I hope, captured your heart as well.

Thank you, Lord, Almighty, Omnipotent One.
You, who are the beauty of all things beautiful,
have captured my wandering heart.
You are the light of my eyes,
the healer of my restless soul,
the one who lifts me up from the depths.
Thank you for your love.
You love me despite my unrighteousness,
with a love that takes away sin.
You love me in my infirmity,
with a love that makes me whole.
Let me receive this unique gift of love,
to drink daily from the fountain of your Spirit.
Thank you, Lord, Almighty, Omnipotent One.
Amen.

St. Augustine of Hippo (354–430) was a theologian, philosopher, and the bishop of Hippo Regius (in what is now Algeria) in North Africa. A convert to Catholicism, Augustine is one of the original four Doctors of the Church and helped lay the foundation of modern Christianity with his writings, which include *Confessions*, *The City of God*, and *On Christian Doctrine*.

30 DAYS
with a **GREAT** Spiritual Teacher

Each book in the 30 Days with a Great Spiritual Teacher series provides a month of daily readings from one of Christianity's most beloved spiritual guides. For each day there is a brief and accessible morning meditation drawn from the mystic's writings, a simple mantra for use throughout the day, and a night prayer to focus one's thoughts as the day ends. These easy-to-use books are the perfect prayer companion for busy people who want to root their spiritual practice in the solid ground of these great spiritual teachers.

TITLES IN THE SERIES INCLUDE:

All Will Be Well (Julian of Norwich)
Come into the Silence (Thomas Merton)
Draw Ever Closer (Henri J. M. Nouwen)
Let Nothing Disturb You (Teresa of Avila)
Let There Be Light (Hildegard of Bingen)
Peace of Heart (Francis of Assisi)
Rejoice in the Lord (Augustine of Hippo)
Set Aside Every Fear (Catherine of Siena)
Set Your Heart Free (Francis de Sales)
Simply Surrender (Thérèse of Lisieux)
True Serenity (Thomas à Kempis)
Where Only Love Can Go (Author of the Cloud of Unknowing)
You Shall Not Want (Author of the Psalms)

**Look for the titles in this series wherever books and eBooks are sold.
Visit avemariapress.com for more information.**